Ultimate STICKER Puzzles

by Tony and Tony Tallarico
cover and sticker illustrations by Cameron Eagle

PSS!
PRICE STERN SLOAN

Interiors copyright © 2005 by Tony and Tony Tallarico.
Cover and sticker illustrations copyright © 2005 by Cameron Eagle.
All rights reserved. Published by Price Stern Sloan, a division of Penguin Young Readers Group, 345 Hudson Street, New York, New York 10014. *PSS!* is a trademark of Penguin Group (USA) Inc.
Printed in China

ISBN 978-0-8431-7737-4   15

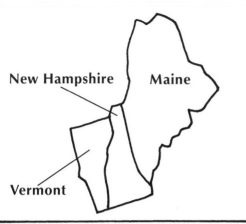

New Hampshire
Maine
Vermont

New England States

The six states that make up the area known as New England are located in the northeastern corner of the United States.

Discover the capital city of each of these three New England states by following the correct path through this maze.

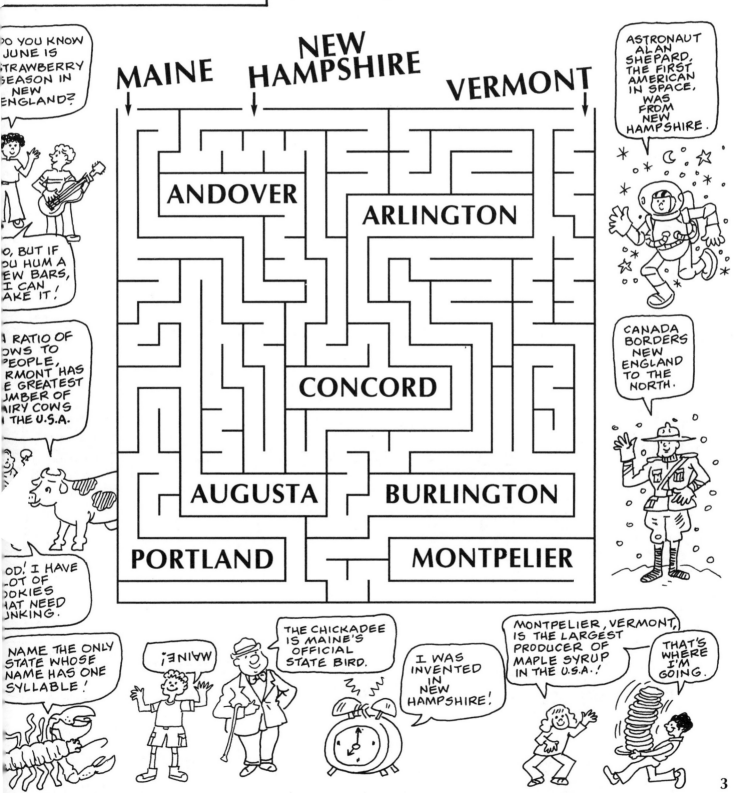

MAINE   NEW HAMPSHIRE   VERMONT

ANDOVER   ARLINGTON

CONCORD

AUGUSTA   BURLINGTON

PORTLAND   MONTPELIER

DO YOU KNOW JUNE IS STRAWBERRY SEASON IN NEW ENGLAND?

NO, BUT IF YOU HUM A FEW BARS, I CAN FAKE IT!

A RATIO OF COWS TO PEOPLE, VERMONT HAS THE GREATEST NUMBER OF DAIRY COWS IN THE U.S.A.

GOOD! I HAVE A LOT OF COOKIES THAT NEED DUNKING.

NAME THE ONLY STATE WHOSE NAME HAS ONE SYLLABLE!

MAINE!

THE CHICKADEE IS MAINE'S OFFICIAL STATE BIRD.

I WAS INVENTED IN NEW HAMPSHIRE!

ASTRONAUT ALAN SHEPARD, THE FIRST AMERICAN IN SPACE, WAS FROM NEW HAMPSHIRE.

CANADA BORDERS NEW ENGLAND TO THE NORTH.

MONTPELIER, VERMONT, IS THE LARGEST PRODUCER OF MAPLE SYRUP IN THE U.S.A.!

THAT'S WHERE I'M GOING.

3

New England States

New England is rich in early Colonial American history. Many of the original European settlers of the 1600s made this area their home.

Unscramble the following historical fact by writing the letter of the alphabet that comes before each letter in the space. We've done the first one for you.

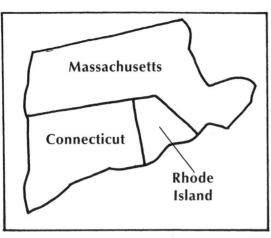

Massachusetts
Connecticut
Rhode Island

THE FIRST TELEPHONE BOOK WAS ISSUED IN CONNECTICUT.

THE FIRST CIRCUS IN THE U.S.A. WAS IN RHODE ISLAND.

CONNECTICUT IS HOME TO THE FIRST HAMBURGER!
YUM!

B
C F D B V T F   J U   X B T

E J G G J D V M U   U P   N B L F

B   M J W J O H   G S P N

G B S N J O H '   N B O Z

T F U U M F S T   I B S O F T T F E

X B U F S   Q P X F S   B O E

F T U B C M J T I F E   H S B J O

N J M M T   B O E   T B X N J M M T .

THE FIG NEWTON WAS NAMED AFTER NEWTON, MASSACHUSETTS.

THE FIRST THANKSGIVING WAS CELEBRATED IN PLYMOUTH, MASSACHUSETTS.

RHODE ISLAND IS THE SMALLEST STATE IN SIZE IN THE U.S.A.!

BASKETBALL WAS INVENTED IN MASSACHUSETTS!

RHODE ISLAND IS HOME TO THE TENNIS HALL OF FAME.

Northeastern States

These three neighboring Northeastern states include New York, otherwise known as the Empire State.

Here is a list of 10 things, each about New York. Write them in the correct spaces. We've done one of them for you.

Albany
Big Apple
Bluebird
Broadway
Long Island
Manhattan
Niagara Falls
Rose
Statue of Liberty
Subway

NEW JERSEY IS A MAJOR SEAPORT STATE.

PHILADELPHIA, PENNSYLVANIA, IS HOME TO THE LIBERTY BELL.

NEW JERSEY HAS THE MOST DINERS IN THE WORLD.

PENNSYLVANIA IS THE FIRST STATE TO LIST THEIR WEBSITE URL ON A LICENSE PLATE.

PUNXSUTAWNEY, PENNSYLVANIA, IS WORLD FAMOUS FOR ITS GROUNDHOG DAY.

NEW JERSEY IS KNOWN AS "THE GARDEN STATE."

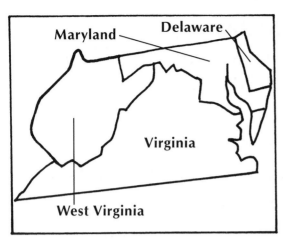

Maryland
Delaware
Virginia
West Virginia

Mid-Atlantic States

This group of states includes Virginia, "the birthplace of a nation."

Write the answer to each clue in the space to the right. Then use your answers to complete the mystery fact below! For example, the letter "N" appears in the spot with a "5" below it. So the space in the mystery fact labeled with a number "5" should be filled in with the letter "N."

West Virginia's nickname "The _____ State" (refers to the rugged Allegheny Mountains)

__ __ __ __ __ __ __ N
10 18 22 20 24 15 23 5

The number of U.S. presidents born in the state of Virginia

__ __ __ H __
4 16 1 27 17

New York Yankee baseball legend nicknamed the Bambino (who was born in Baltimore, Maryland)

__ __ __ __   __ __ __ H
6 15 21 3   11 19 9 27

The first state to ratify the United States Constitution (thus becoming the very first state)

__ __ __ A __ __ __ __
13 26 8 15 14 25 2 7

MYSTERY FACT:

__ __ __ __ __ __ __ __ __ ,   __ A __ Y L __ N __ ,
1 2 3 4 5 6 7 8 9   10   11   12   13

__ __ S   T H E   F __ R S __
14 15   16   17

WE DIDN'T KNOW THAT... DID YOU ?

C __ M M __ __ I T Y   I N   T H E
18   19 20

U. S.   __ __ __ L __   A S   A
21 22 23   24

P L __ N N __ D   C I T Y .
25   26

6

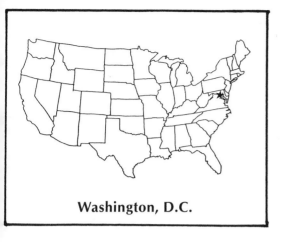

Washington, D.C.

The Nation's Capital

Washington, D.C., the seat of the U.S. government, is not a state. It has been our nation's capital since 1790. "D.C." stands for "District of Columbia."

Below is a list of words about Washington, D.C. Can you find each word in the puzzle grid and circle it? The words may read up and down, from side to side, diagonally, or backward.

Once you have circled all of the words, shade or color in each circle. Only a few letters in the grid should remain uncolored. Beginning in the top left corner of the grid and moving across each row from left to right, list each of the remaining, uncolored letters in the spaces below. They will spell out the answer to the surprise trivia question! We've filled in the first and last letters for you.

- ○ CAPITOL
- ○ CITY
- ○ GARDENS
- ○ HISTORIC
- ○ LIBRARY
- ○ MEMORIALS
- ○ MONUMENTS
- ○ MUSEUMS
- ○ NATIONAL MALL
- ○ PARKS
- ○ PENTAGON
- ○ POTOMAC
- ○ TOURISM
- ○ WHITE HOUSE

W	P	P	I	E	H	C	M	R
H	A	C	A	P	I	T	O	L
I	R	A	R	T	S	G	N	L
T	K	M	Y	E	T	A	U	A
E	S	O	R	C	O	R	M	M
H	L	T	A	H	R	D	E	L
O	A	O	R	A	I	E	N	A
U	I	P	B	R	C	N	T	N
S	R	L	I	E	S	S	S	O
E	O	L	L	E	N	F	A	I
N	M	M	S	I	R	U	O	T
P	E	N	T	A	G	O	N	A
T	M	U	S	E	U	M	S	N

BE SURE TO STOP BY AND VISIT.

Name the Frenchman who designed the American capital.

P _ _ _ _ _ _   _ _ _ _ _ _ _   _ ' _ _ _ _ _ T

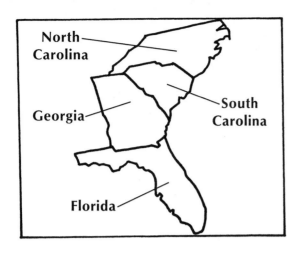

Southeastern States

These four Southeastern states all border the Atlantic Ocean, thus offering vacationers many miles of sandy beaches.

Can you match each of these beaches to its home state by finding the correct path through the maze?

ALTHOUGH IT MAY APPEAR TO BE... FLORIDA IS NOT THE SOUTHERNMOST STATE... HAWAII IS!

SOUTH CAROLINA BECAME A STATE ON MAY 23, 1788.

BLACKBEARD ISLAND IS LOCATED OFF THE COAST OF GEORGIA!

KRISPY KREME DOUGHNUTS WAS FOUNDED IN WINSTON-SALEM, NORTH CAROLINA.

IN 1903, THE WRIGHT BROTHERS MADE THE FIRST POWERED FLIGHT BY MAN AT KILL DEVIL HILL NEAR KITTY HAWK, NORTH CAROLINA.

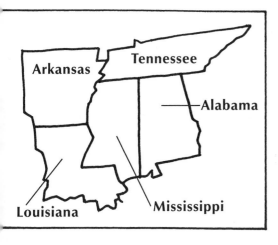

Southern States

Frontiersman Davy Crockett wasn't born on a mountaintop in Tennessee (as the famous song suggests). He was born on the banks of Limestone Creek, in northeastern Tennessee.

Unscramble the answer to each clue. Then write the circled letters in the spaces below in the order they appear to complete the mystery fact. We've done the first one for you.

CLUES	SCRAMBLED LETTERS	UNSCRAMBLED WORDS
French name for a slow-moving river	A B Y O U	B A Y (O) U
Official state tree of Arkansas	N E P I	_ (O) _ _
U.S. president from Arkansas	O T L I C N N	_ (O) _ _ (O) _ (O)
Alabama's official nut	N P C E A	_ _ _ _ (O)
Soft drink Edward Barq first bottled in Mississippi	O R T O E B R E	_ (O) _ (O) _ (O)(O) _
Famous Louisiana celebration	I A M R D A R G S	_ _ (O)(O) _ _ (O) _ _

MYSTERY FACT:

K N (O) X V _ _ _ L E , _ E _ _ E S S E E ,

H _ S _ _ _ D T H _ 1 9 8 2

W O _ L _ ' S F A I _ .

LET'S GO!

I'M ON MY WAY!

WAIT FOR ME!

I'M MOVING AS FAST AS I CAN.

I'LL MEET YOU THERE!

THIS WAY

...OR THIS WAY

KEEP OFF THE GRASS

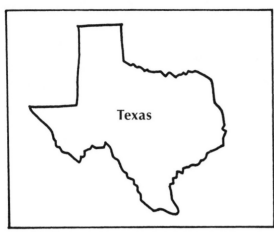

Texas

Southern States

Texas, popularly known as the Lone Star State, is the leading oil producer in the U.S.A.

Can you solve this Texas crossword puzzle?

THE MANNED SPACECRAFT CENTER IS NEAR HOUSTON, TEXAS.

ACROSS

1. State abbreviation
3. Soft drink invented in Texas
   Dr _____
4. Texas is the _____ largest state
6. Football's Dallas _____
7. Texas capital city
8. Hot pepper that originated in Texas

TEXAS, HAWAII, AND VERMONT ARE THE ONLY STATES THAT WERE ONCE INDEPENDENT REPUBLICS.

DOWN

1. Popular historic site in San Antonio
2. Official small state mammal, which eats insects
5. Last name of famous Texan or home city to baseball's Astros

Northern States

These two Northern states border Lake Superior (the largest of the Great Lakes).

In the code box below, each numeral stands for a letter of the alphabet. For example, "2" stands for the letter "F." Using the code box, write the correct letter in each numbered space to decode this fact about Wisconsin.

9	21	18	14	4	2	22	17	10	23	16	3	6
A	B	C	D	E	F	G	H	I	J	K	L	M
19	7	12	24	1	8	5	11	15	20	25	13	26
N	O	P	Q	R	S	T	U	V	W	X	Y	Z

20 10 8 18 7 19 8 10 19   10 8   5 17 4

14 9 10 1 13   18 9 12 10 5 9 3   7 2

5 17 4   11 8 .   10 5

12 1 7 14 11 18 4 8   6 7 1 4

6 10 3 16   5 17 9 19   9 19 13

7 5 17 4 1   8 5 9 5 4 .

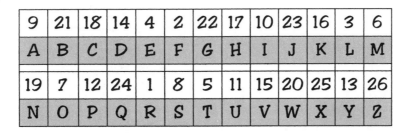

11

Use the license plate stickers to keep track of the plates you see along the road! Can you find all 51 license plates?

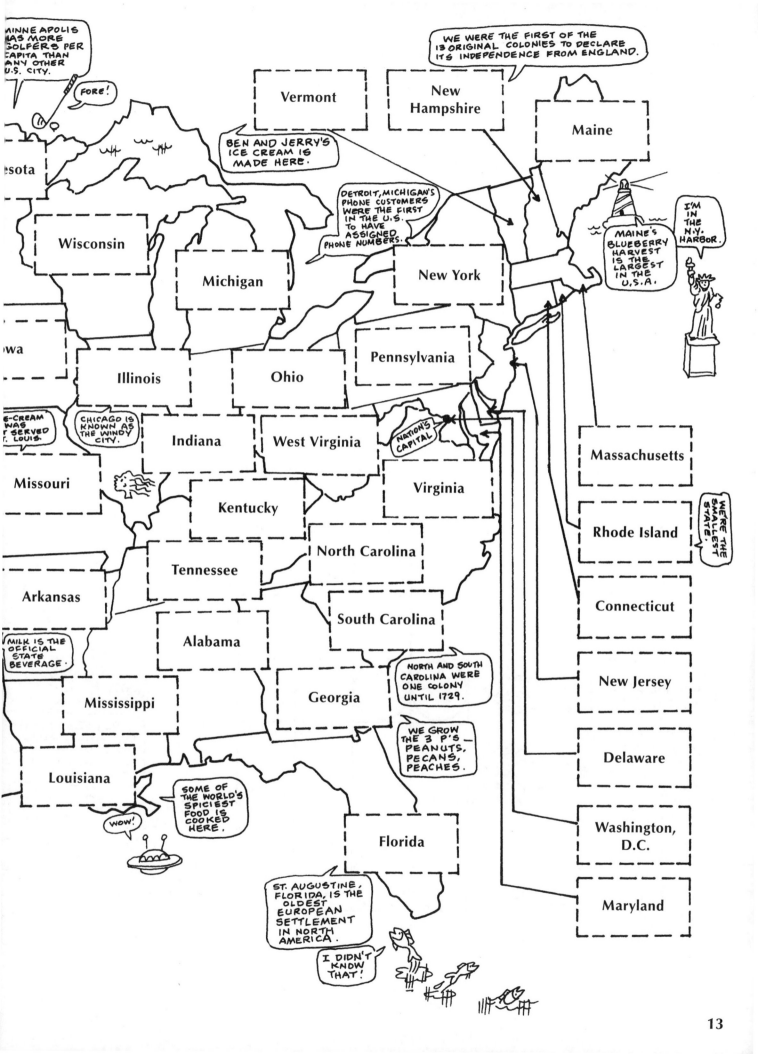

13

Midwestern States

These Midwestern states include Illinois, home to the Sears Tower, which is the tallest building on the North American continent.

Solve this picture crossword puzzle. Then, at the bottom of the page, place each circled letter in its corresponding numbered space. You will reveal the name of the capital of Illinois.

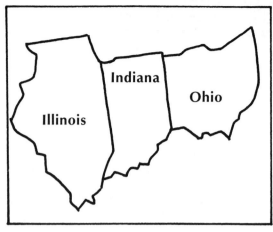

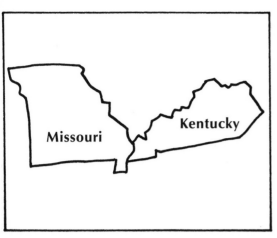

Midwestern States

It was at the 1904 St. Louis World's Fair (in Missouri) that tea with ice was first served.

Drop a letter from every word in Column A to form a new word for Column B. Write the dropped letters in the oval spaces to form the name of the person who invented iced tea. We've done the first one for you.

COLUMN A:	COLUMN B:	INVENTOR:
RICE	ICE	R
HEIR		
CLOSE		
HAIR		
RAISE		
REEL		
DART		
BALL		
LONE		
BEAN		
CORE		
HOLD		
YEAST		
DRAW		
HEAD		
NARROW		

THE SONG "HAPPY BIRTHDAY TO YOU" WAS WRITTEN BY TWO SISTERS FROM KENTUCKY!

THE FIRST SUCCESSFUL PARACHUTE JUMP FROM AN AIRPLANE WAS MADE IN MISSOURI!

THE KENTUCKY DERBY IS THE OLDEST CONTINUOUSLY HELD HORSE RACE IN THE U.S.A.!

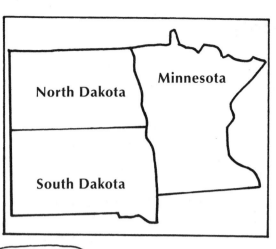

Midwestern States

North Dakota and South Dakota both became states on the same day—November 2, 1889.

Travel through this maze to discover when Minnesota became a state.

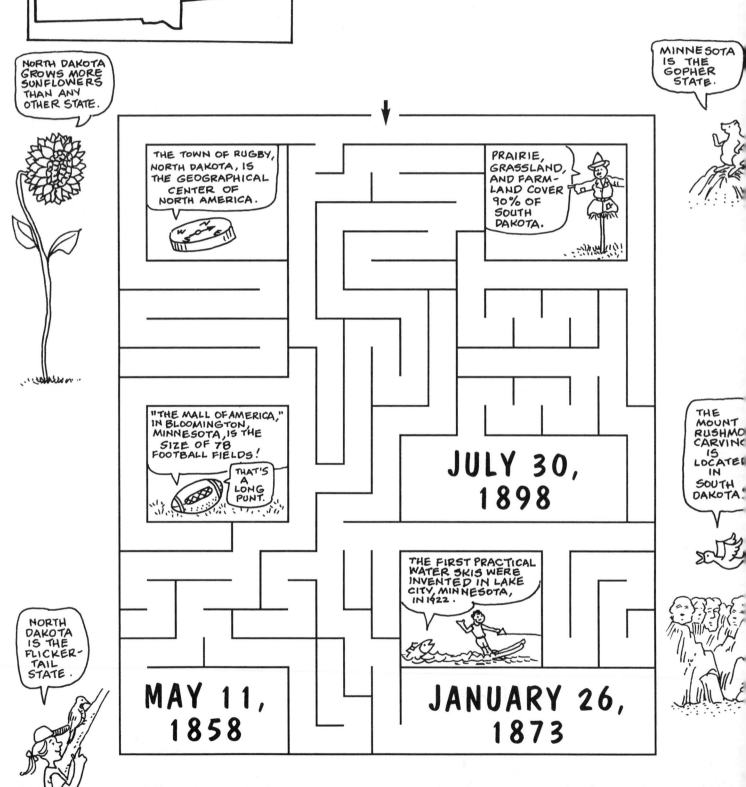

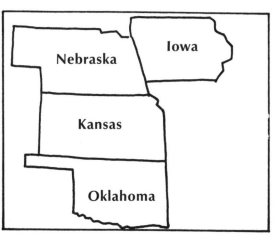

Midwestern States

Did you know that the world's first parking meter was installed in Oklahoma City, Oklahoma, in 1935? Below, cross out all of the odd-numbered boxes. Then starting with the first row across, list the remaining letters in the spaces below in the order they appear. You'll reveal another mystery fact about Oklahoma!

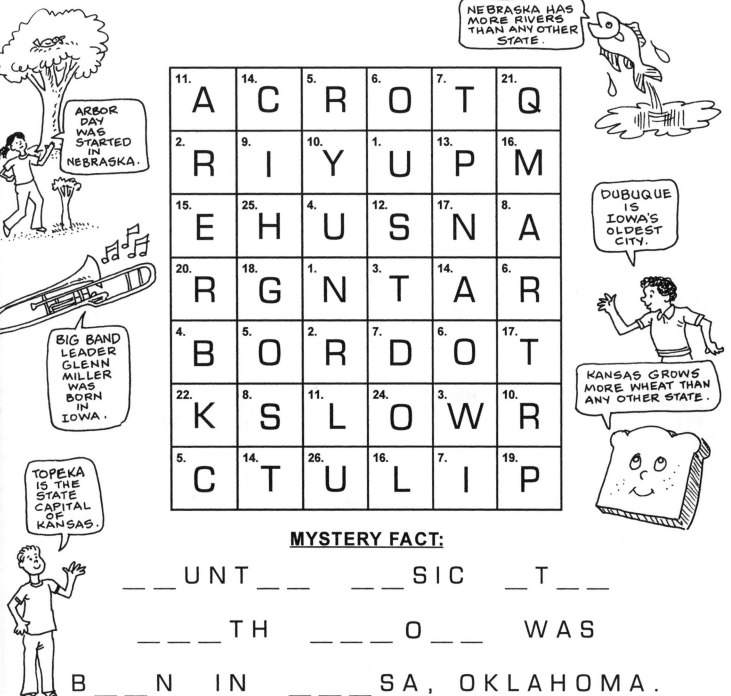

11. A	14. C	5. R	6. O	7. T	21. Q
2. R	9. I	10. Y	1. U	13. P	16. M
15. E	25. H	4. U	12. S	17. N	8. A
20. R	18. G	1. N	3. T	14. A	6. R
4. B	5. O	2. R	7. D	6. O	17. T
22. K	8. S	11. L	24. O	3. W	10. R
5. C	14. T	26. U	16. L	7. I	19. P

MYSTERY FACT:

_ _ U N T _ _   _ _ S I C   _ T _ _

_ _ _ T H   _ _ _ O _ _   W A S

B _ _ N   I N   _ _ _ S A ,   O K L A H O M A .

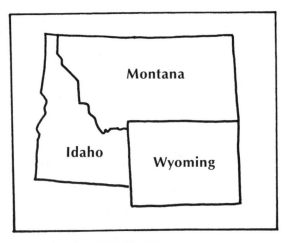

Western States

Yellowstone National Park covers more than two million acres and is so big that it runs through all three of these Western states.

Use word wheels A and B to complete the corresponding facts about Yellowstone. Starting at the arrow and moving clockwise, write every other letter in the blank spaces. Go around each circle twice. We've filled in the first letter in each fact for you to get you started.

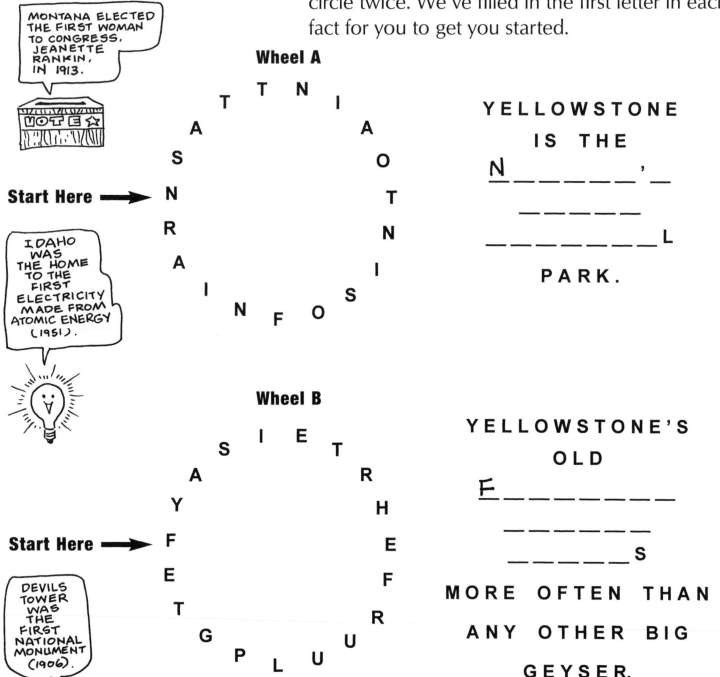

MONTANA ELECTED THE FIRST WOMAN TO CONGRESS, JEANETTE RANKIN, IN 1913.

IDAHO WAS THE HOME TO THE FIRST ELECTRICITY MADE FROM ATOMIC ENERGY (1951).

DEVILS TOWER WAS THE FIRST NATIONAL MONUMENT (1906).

Wheel A

Start Here →

YELLOWSTONE IS THE

N _ _ _ _ _ _ , _

_ _ _ _ _

_ _ _ _ _ _ _ _ L

PARK.

Wheel B

Start Here →

YELLOWSTONE'S OLD

F _ _ _ _ _ _ _

_ _ _ _ _ _

_ _ _ _ _ S

MORE OFTEN THAN

ANY OTHER BIG

GEYSER.

Western States

These three mountainous states offer some of the most breathtaking views in the country.

To discover which state is home to the Rocky Mountains, travel through the correct maze path.

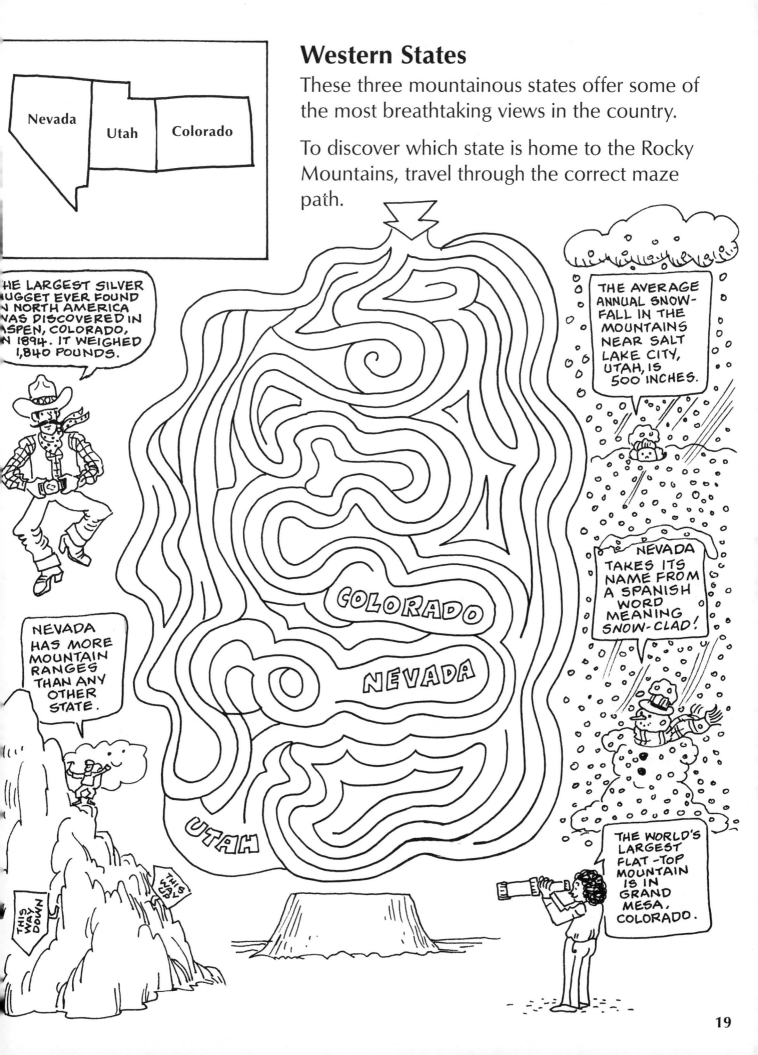

Nevada

Utah   Colorado

THE LARGEST SILVER NUGGET EVER FOUND IN NORTH AMERICA WAS DISCOVERED IN ASPEN, COLORADO, IN 1894. IT WEIGHED 1,840 POUNDS.

NEVADA HAS MORE MOUNTAIN RANGES THAN ANY OTHER STATE.

THE AVERAGE ANNUAL SNOW-FALL IN THE MOUNTAINS NEAR SALT LAKE CITY, UTAH, IS 500 INCHES.

NEVADA TAKES ITS NAME FROM A SPANISH WORD MEANING SNOW-CLAD!

THE WORLD'S LARGEST FLAT-TOP MOUNTAIN IS IN GRAND MESA, COLORADO.

COLORADO

NEVADA

UTAH

THIS WAY DOWN

THIS WAY

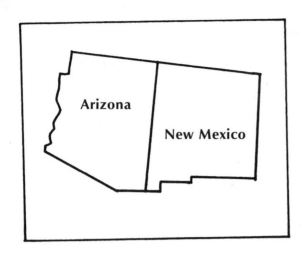

Southwestern States

These Southwestern states offer many natural wonders, such as the Grand Canyon (in Arizona) and the Rio Grande (New Mexico's longest river).

Unscramble the following fact by writing the letter of the alphabet that comes *before* each of these scrambled letters. We've done the first one for you.

THE "ORGAN PIPE CACTUS NATIONAL MONUMENT" IS IN ARIZONA!

OH, OH!

"EL CAMINO REAL" IS THE LONGEST ROAD IN THE U.S.!

IT WAS FIRST TRAVELED IN 1598.

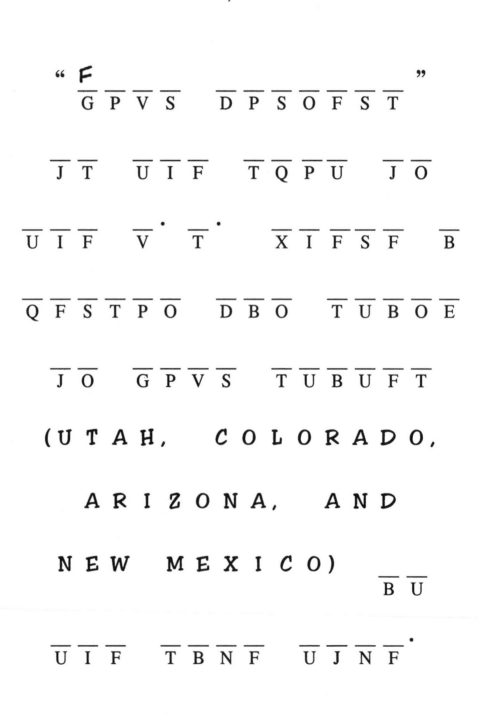

" F _ _ _   _ _ _ _ _ _ _ "
  G P V S D P S O F S T

_ _   _ _ _   _ _ _ _   _ _
J T U I F T Q P U J O

_ _ _   _ . _ .   _ _ _ _ _   _
U I F V T X I F S F B

_ _ _ _ _ _   _ _ _   _ _ _ _ _
Q F S T P O D B O T U B O E

_ _   _ _ _ _   _ _ _ _ _ _
J O G P V S T U B U F T

(UTAH, COLORADO,

ARIZONA, AND

NEW MEXICO) _ _
                B U

_ _ _   _ _ _ _   _ _ _ _ .
U I F T B N F U J N F

20

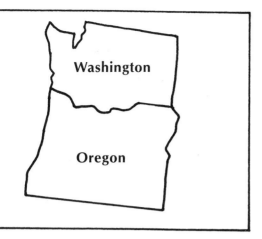

West Coast States

Washington and Oregon make up the Pacific Northwest region of the United States.

Below is a list of words about Washington, which is the only state to be named after a president. Can you find each word in the puzzle grid and circle it? The words may read up and down, from side to side, diagonally, or backward. Once you have circled all of the words, shade or color in each circle. Only a few letters in the grid should remain uncolored. Beginning in the top left corner of the grid and moving across each row from left to right, list each of the remaining, uncolored letters in the spaces below. They will spell out the state's nickname! We've filled in the first letter for you.

- ☐ BEACHES
- ☐ COAST
- ☐ FARMS
- ☐ FORESTS
- ☐ HIKING
- ☐ HISTORY
- ☐ KENT
- ☐ MOUNT RAINIER
- ☐ OLYMPIA
- ☐ SCENIC
- ☐ SEATTLE
- ☐ SKIING
- ☐ SPACE NEEDLE
- ☐ SPOKANE
- ☐ TIMBER
- ☐ WILDLIFE

R	E	F	I	L	D	L	I	W
E	L	A	O	E	V	E	R	G
I	D	R	L	R	B	H	E	N
N	E	M	Y	E	E	I	L	I
I	E	S	M	B	A	S	T	I
A	N	T	P	M	C	T	T	K
R	E	N	I	I	H	O	A	S
T	C	E	A	T	E	R	E	C
N	A	K	G	R	S	Y	S	E
U	P	G	N	I	K	I	H	N
O	S	P	O	K	A	N	E	I
M	E	E	N	T	S	A	O	C

THE _ _ _ _ _ _ _ _ _ STATE.

21

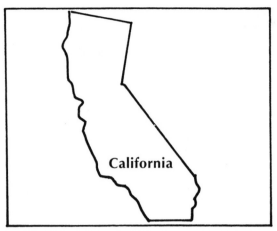

California

West Coast States

"The Golden State" stretches along the Pacific Ocean from the bottom of Oregon to the top of Mexico.

Can you solve this California crossword puzzle?

THE OROVILLE DAM IS THE HIGHEST IN THE U.S. (754 FEET).

THE STATE LIES ON THE SAN ANDREAS FAULT LINE.

EARTH-QUAKE!

THE TALLEST LIVING THINGS ARE HERE... REDWOOD TREES.

Across

2. ____ Francisco
4. California's largest city Los _____
5. California is in the _____ Time Zone
6. State tree: California _____
7. Southern California amphitheater the Hollywood ____

Down

1. Continent's highest waterfall Yosemite _____
3. Capital city
7. State animal, the Grizzly ____

WE GROW THE MOST FRUITS AND VEGETABLES OF ANY U.S. STATE!

THE MOJAVE DESERT IS HERE.

Non-Contiguous States

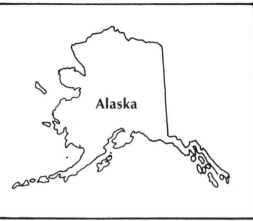

So, what's a non-contiguous state anyway? It means that state's borders don't touch those of any other state. Alaska, although part of North America, is separated from the continental United States by Canada. And Hawaii is a cluster of six islands located in the Pacific Ocean.

USE THIS CHART TO DECODE THE MESSAGE.

	1	2	3	4	5	6
A	W	C	I	L	S	M
B	O	U	T	H	F	L
C	N	A	D	R	E	K

ALOHA! HAVE FUN.

$\overset{I}{\underline{A3}}\ \overline{C1}$ $\overline{B4}\ \overline{C2}\ \overline{A1}\ \overline{C2}\ \overline{A3}\ \overline{A3}$' $\overline{B3}\ \overline{B4}\ \overline{C5}$

$\overline{A2}\ \overline{B1}\ \overline{C1}\ \overline{B3}\ \overline{A3}\ \overline{C1}\ \overline{C5}\ \overline{C1}\ \overline{B3}\ \overline{C2}\ \overline{A4}$

$\overline{B2}\ \overline{C1}\ \overline{A3}\ \overline{B3}\ \overline{C5}\ \overline{C3}$ $\overline{A5}\ \overline{B3}\ \overline{C2}\ \overline{B3}\ \overline{C5}\ \overline{A5}$ $\overline{A3}\ \overline{A5}$

$\overline{C4}\ \overline{C5}\ \overline{B5}\ \overline{C5}\ \overline{C4}\ \overline{C4}\ \overline{C5}\ \overline{C3}$ $\overline{B3}\ \overline{B1}$ $\overline{C2}\ \overline{A5}$

"$\overline{B3}\ \overline{B4}\ \overline{C5}$ $\overline{A6}\ \overline{C2}\ \overline{A3}\ \overline{C1}\ \overline{B6}\ \overline{C2}\ \overline{C1}\ \overline{C3}$."

$\overline{A3}\ \overline{C1}$ $\overline{C2}\ \overline{A4}\ \overline{C2}\ \overline{A5}\ \overline{C6}\ \overline{C2}$' $\overline{B3}\ \overline{B4}\ \overline{C5}$

$\overline{B2}$. $\overline{A5}$. $\overline{A3}\ \overline{A5}$ $\overline{C4}\ \overline{C5}\ \overline{B5}\ \overline{C5}\ \overline{C4}\ \overline{C4}\ \overline{C5}\ \overline{C3}$

"$\overline{B3}\ \overline{B1}$ $\overline{C2}\ \overline{A5}$ $\overline{B3}\ \overline{B4}\ \overline{C5}$ $\overline{A4}\ \overline{B1}\ \overline{A1}\ \overline{C5}\ \overline{C4}$ 4 8 ."

23

Answer Key

Page 3

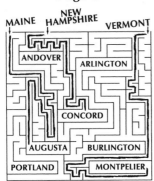

MAINE NEW HAMPSHIRE VERMONT
ANDOVER ARLINGTON
CONCORD
AUGUSTA BURLINGTON
PORTLAND MONTPELIER

Page 4

BECAUSE IT WAS
CFDBVTF JU XBT

DIFFICULT TO MAKE
EJGGJDVMU UP NBLF

A LIVING FROM
B MJWJOH GSPN

FARMING, MANY
GBSNJOH, NBOZ

SETTLERS HARNESSED
TFUUMFST IBSOFTTFE

WATER POWER AND
XBUFS QPXFS BOE

ESTABLISHED GRAIN
FTUBCMJTIFE HSBJO

MILLS AND SAWMILLS.
NJMMT BOE TBXNJMMT.

Page 5

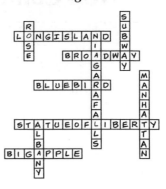

ROSE, LONGISLAND, SUBWAY, BROADWAY, CENTRALPARK, BLUEBIRD, MANHATTAN, STATUEOFLIBERTY, ALBANY, BIGAPPLE

Page 6

MOUNTAIN
10 18 22 20 24 15 23 5

EIGHT
4 16 1 27 17

BABE RUTH
6 15 21 3 11 19 9 27

DELAWARE
13 26 8 15 14 25 2 7

Page 6 (cont.)

MYSTERY FACT:

GREENBELT, MARYLAND,
1 2 3 4 5 6 7 8 9   10 11   12 13

WAS THE FIRST
14 15   16 17

COMMUNITY IN THE
18 19 20

U.S. BUILT AS A
21 22 23 24

PLANNED CITY.
25   26

Page 7

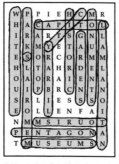

WHITEHOUSE, PARKS, ISLAIROL, PIECAPMYECHARBLLEN, CAPITOL, SIGNMONUMENTS, ARTGARDENFAI, MSIRUOT, PENTAGON, MUSEUMS

PIERRE CHARLES L'ENFANT

Page 8

DAYTONA BEACH MYRTLE BEACH CASWELL BEACH ST. SIMONS BEACH
SOUTH CAROLINA
GEORGIA
NORTH CAROLINA
FLORIDA

Page 9

UNSCRAMBLED WORDS

BAYOU
PINE
CLINTON
PECAN
ROOT BEER
MARDI GRAS

KNOXVILLE, TENNESSEE,
HOSTED THE 1982
WORLD'S FAIR.

Page 10

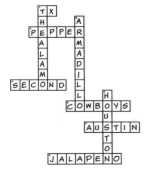

TX
THE
PEPPER ARMADILLO
ALAMO
SECOND
COWBOYS HOUSTON
AUSTIN
JALAPENO

Page 11

WISCONSIN IS THE
20 10 8 11 9 18 10 19   10 8   19 5

DAIRY CAPITAL OF
14 9 10 1 18   18 9 12 10 5 9 3   7 2

THE U.S. IT
5 17 4   11 8   10 5

PRODUCES MORE
12 1 7 14 11 18 4 8   6 7 1 4

MILK THAN ANY
6 10 3 16   5 17 9 19   9 19 19

OTHER STATE.
7 5 17 4 1   8 5 9 5 4

Page 14

DRUM, UMBRELLA, PENCIL, GIFT, FISH, NOSE, EIGHT, HOSE
SPRINGFIELD
9 2 3 7 11 6 10 4 5 1

Page 15

COLUMN A:	COLUMN B:	INVENTOR:
RICE	ICE	R
HEIR	HER	I
CLOSE	LOSE	C
HAIR	AIR	H
RAISE	RISE	A
REEL	EEL	R
DART	ART	D
BALL	ALL	B
LONE	ONE	L
BEAN	BAN	E
CORE	ORE	C
HOLD	OLD	H
YEAST	EAST	Y
DRAW	RAW	D
HEAD	HAD	E
NARROW	ARROW	N

Page 16

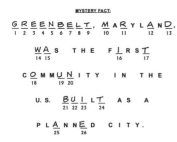

THE TOWN OF RUGBY, NORTH DAKOTA, IS THE GEOGRAPHICAL CENTER OF NORTH AMERICA.

PRAIRIE, GRASSLAND, AND FARM LAND COVER 90% OF SOUTH DAKOTA.

THE FALL OF AMERICA, A BLACKSMITHING BUSINESS, IS THE SIZE OF 110 FOOTBALL FIELDS.

THE FIRST FRACTIONAL PATCH SKATING OF 10% OF HORSE FARMERS IS ON LAKE OAHE.

JULY 30, 1898
MAY 11, 1858
JANUARY 26, 1873

Page 17

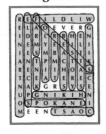

(grid with X marks and letters: CROX, RYYM, USKA, RGXAR, BXRXOX, KSXOWR, XTULXX)

MYSTERY FACT:
COUNTRY MUSIC STAR
GARTH BROOKS WAS
BORN IN TULSA, OKLAHOMA.

Page 18

YELLOWSTONE
IS THE
NATION'S
FIRST
NATIONAL
PARK.
YELLOWSTONE'S
OLD
FAITHFUL
GEYSER
ERUPTs
MORE OFTEN THAN
ANY OTHER BIG
GEYSER.

Page 19

COLORADO, NEVADA, UTAH

Page 20

"FOUR CORNERS"
GPVS DPSOFST

IS THE SPOT IN
JT UIF TQPU JO

THE U.S. WHERE A
UIF V T   XIFSF B

PERSON CAN STAND
QFSTPO DBO TUBOE

IN FOUR STATES
JO GPVS TUBUFT

(UTAH, COLORADO,
ARIZONA, AND
NEW MEXICO) AT
BU
THE SAME TIME.
UIF TBNF UJNF

Page 21

REFILLDLIW, ELEVERG, NEMYBELLI, IASMBASTTK, TPMCTIHOSAE, AKGRGGRS, NGNIKIHN, SPOKANE, MEENTSAOC

THE EVERGREEN STATE.

Page 22

FALL, SAN, LOS ANGELES, SACRAMENTO, PACIFIC, REDWOOD, BOWL, BEAR

Page 23

	1	2	3	4	5	6
A	W	C	I	L	S	M
B	O	U	T	H	F	L
C	N	A	D	R	E	K

IN HAWAII, THE
A3 C1   B4 C2   A4 B2 C5

CONTINENTAL
A1 B1 C1 B3 A2 C1 A2 B1 C1 A4

UNITED STATES IS
B2 C1 A3 C3 B1 C3   A3 B3 C1 B3 C5   A3 A3

REFERRED TO AS
C4 C5 B5 C5 C4 C4 C1   B3 A1   A4 A3

"THE MAINLAND."
B1 C3   B3 C4 A3 A1 A2 A1 A1 C1

IN ALASKA THE
A3 C1   A2 C1 A4 A3 C2 A2   B1 C3

U.S. IS REFERRED
B2   A3 A3   C4 C5 B5 C5 C4 C4 C1

TO AS "THE LOWER 48."
B3 B1   A4 A3   B1 C3   C1 A1 B4 C5 C4